Maddie Garcia

A Vision of
She

Wider Perspectives Publishing ¤ 2022 ¤ Hampton Roads, Va

Editing services provided by Crickyt J. Meyer
Copyright © January 2022, Maddie Garcia
Wider Perspectives Publishing, Hampton Roads, Va
ISBN: 978-1-952773-50-1

From the Author:

This collection of poems is very dear to my heart. They illustrate some of my journey to self-love and self-discovery, but also the path to knowing what unconditional love feels and looks like: It's *She*. Becoming a mother is probably one of the biggest events in any woman's life, but having a daughter, changed how I viewed my own life. It made me take a hard look at myself and the example I wanted to set for my baby girl. Looking into her eyes, I just knew I had to try and be the best version of me, for us. Motherhood taught me that being a good parent is not telling your children what to do but letting them see it day in and day out, reflected in you. Some of the poems are inspired by and focused on other young ladies who, by request or out of love, will find themselves on paper. To be a She is beautiful and deserves celebrating, even the tough milestones. One of the sweetest realizations putting this project together is that She is as much Me as She is Them; I hope that as you read you can find a bit of yourself too.

There are 30 poems in this book. The meaning of the number 30 expresses how I feel about every word written here. The number 3 signifies self-expression, enthusiasm, inspiration, and creativity. The number 0 is a symbol of infinity, wholeness, flow, and cycles. Bound together as the number 30, they represent creativity, optimism, tolerance, socializing, imagination, and inspiration.

I will forever be thankful for falling in love with words and the creative outlet that relationship gave me. I never thought I would have the opportunity to immortalize my words, to give them the power to live far after I am gone. I could not have done this without the support of my family, friends and all my 757 poets that serve as an inspiration and push me to want to better my craft as a wordsmith. To everyone who had a little something to do with bringing this project to life, thank you from the bottom of my heart.

Enjoy,
-*Maddie*

Contents

Chapter 3: There is Nothing I Would Change

Chapter 4: May She Feel Special in Every Way

For Her...

Maddie Garcia

For Her

To the bully, who tried to break her:
Little did you know that every punch
was knocking down walls
to reveal the heart of a fighter.
But this poem is not for you.

This poem is for her.

For all those times
She had to bite her tongue,
swallow her words,
forced to wear spitballs like bows decorating her beautiful hair,

For those times her body was kicked down the stairs,
landing against the wall, ashamed,
never prepared for the echo of laughter that followed,

For all those times she wished she was never there,
wiping tears from her eyes
because she was sure that nobody cared,

For her.

Because deep down it still hurts,
not being able to make sense of all the hate,
hate for being different,
hate for not speaking the language.

There was this world between them
and not enough time to put together
the "I don't like her"
with "Why can't we be friends?"

She had to learn
that courage is found right next to desperation,
right before the end,
when you have to ball your fist
and protect your self-respect.

For standing up to her bully,
No. Longer. Afraid.
For the strong woman she became.

She had to learn
to nurture the fragile child inside of herself,
who will never understand.

For being a survivor,
For loving herself,
This poem, this poem. This poem!
This poem is for her.

Maddie Garcia

Super

I can't remember when it happened
but I fell in,
got sucked in like Alice,
wondering,

Innocently thinking my reflection
should look like the girls in magazines,

Thinking that I could dress this body
with the clothing seen on the mannequins,

Only to be crushed 'cause
you can't dress an American girl doll
in Barbie clothing.

Holding my breath-
as if not breathing would somehow be
equivalent to losing inches,
and believing my existence was a tragedy;

that needed fixing.

Fix not the air brushed deceiving images
injected into my psyche, no.

But this universe of fake truths growing inside me,
too fat, too short, too black, too ugly,
the rings around my Saturn tight and unsightly,
an outcast alien form, deformed,
curving from the standardized One Size Fits All
to realizing that I DON'T FIT!

It took me hulking out of my Bruce Banner form to realize
I'm not like them, that there is only one of me
and even though I am Gamora green
I can still be a superhero in someone's Marvel Universe.

Imagine...
loving the thunder in your thighs,
the way your booty bounces in those pants.

Imagine not crying because of what you look like.

I have learned,
my body will shape shift faster than my mind can evolve,
that we must learn to catch up and appreciate our bodies
at whatever stage we find ourselves at.

Shazzam!

Something beautiful always happens
when the superhero inside
learns to love their human counterpart.

Broken Woman

When a broken woman speaks,
She gives pain a voice.
She gives hurt a makeover.
She grows wings of hope.
She empowers!

Translating the stories trapped in every scar,
she reveals the size of her heart,
made strong by the journey.

Her journey,
that today dares to be spoken,
embracing difficulties as tokens,
as experiences that have awoken
the fierce animal she had sleeping inside.
No longer confined!

Now, she looks at the world
with eyes wide open.
Her tears flush out the shame.

Missing pieces allow her light to shine through.
She glows
because she would not be the strong woman she is
if she had never been broken.

Masterpiece

Everyone has a purpose.
That, we should strongly believe.
You would not be on this earth
if there was not a destiny to be fulfilled.

Sometimes, is not about the destination
but the lessons gathered in between,
the resilience and thick exterior one can build.

Thick,
not to block the outside from coming in,
but to build your inside well enough to share it at will.

Confidence is magnetic.
Others will gravitate to it,
not because of how good you look
but how extraordinary you feel.

Little girls need to learn
that they are beautiful, since birth.
Not just because momma and daddy think so,
but because her beauty is innate.
Not dictated by society,
she is beautiful in every way.

Just imagine how the world would be
if every little girl grew up to believe
that the woman they see in the mirror
is perfect, as is,

not waiting until she is older
to see all the years of beauty
that she missed.

My purpose, I strongly believe,
is to make sure every little one knows:
She is,
I am,
We are (SING IT!)
a Masterpiece!

Black Girl Magic

Black Girl Magic...
Is being Afro-Latina and growing up
with a thousand different names
describing the color of my skin,
to later learn
that it doesn't matter what I've been calling it.
I Am It.

Black Girl Magic...
Means learning to love all my parts.
You cannot hide what it is in plain sight and I,
I am beautifully black.

Black Girl Magic...
Means letting go of any shame.
Teaching the little girl inside
that She is beautiful, as is,
not because of what She looks like
but because of what She carries in her heart.

Black Girl Magic...
Is looking in the mirror every day
and reminding myself of that.

Black Girl Magic...
Means pride in what I represent.
It's having the odds stocked against you
and proving them all wrong.

Black Girl Magic...
Is realizing, I am the fight of my ancestors.
That I am flexible and when I bend
I am held together by their experiences,
so I don't break.
Even today, I am kept upright by history
and their strength.
So, I'll be darned if I don't come out every day,
flexing the power of what this melanin represents.
Because, Black Girl Magic can come from any culture,
in a thousand different shades!

Maddie Garcia

Who am I?

I come from a seed imported from a faraway land
to satisfy the colonizer's curiosity of what could blossom
from the inside.
Yet my kind will forever be unknown,
strange fruit that will never be understood.
'Cause I'm a contradiction of what they see,
versus what I taste like,
Bewitching the palate,
Convincing the brain that the eyes have been lying
since the beginning of time.

I am a flower that was deemed to bloom in any garden,
even a concrete one,
like a parasite that attaches to its surroundings not to die.

Survival of the fittest,
I Gloria Gaynor the shit out of this life.
I am a survivor.

A child destined to thrive, to be remembered,
words I immortalized in this poem, so I never forget
I have to stay working hard.

They keep pushing back the finish line,
thinking giving up will be my only choice.
They keep forgetting where I come from.

I am as much colonizer, as I am Taino, as I am slave.
I can muscle my way to the finish line
or verbally slap you with my intellect,
en Español y en Inglés.

Yes,
I get tongue twisted time and again.
But that's from all the verbs I have bending in my head.
I can call you "hijo eh puta" or "son of a bitch"
All in the same breath.

(I'm sorry... Excuse me...
I forget what I was gonna say next.
Concentrate!)

I am concentrated coffee- before it became Americanized,
Café Dominicano.
Like the Caribbean sun, I will always shine.

I am Black girl magic passed down from my black grandma
through my white mom.
To get a clear picture, a mix of different races,
that is how Dominican I am!

I AM
the dopest line in the poem that makes you want to say: REWIND!

I am the exact vision of the future my ancestors had,
the point of reference Next-Generation will always look back at.
I am a mother, a daughter, a poet, a sister, a friend,
a work in progress.
I am the promise to my past that my future would be great,
in the present.
I'm still downloading,
and I can't wait to show you what's next!

Maddie Garcia

An Open Letter to My Insecurities

Dear you,
Those who linger inside of me
the voices, the feelings, the things
always making me believe that
it is never enough,
I am not enough,
that I never will be...
Dear You.

Because,
even pain becomes the norm,
self-doubt a regular thought,
as much as it hurts,
even you--are all dear to me.
I have to admit as much as I hate
all of what you make me feel,
Without you,
I would not be.

What I keep learning as time goes on
Is not to be afraid to take you on.
I may not always win but if I can get past it,
I will be amazed at what I can achieve.

Like reciting the Dominican National Anthem
at kindergarten graduation at the age of 5,
Like wearing the revealing outfit to dance on stage
and shine,
Like reading the words of a poem written by me,
about me, and seeing someone else cry;

I was scared for all of that,
viewed myself failing at it each time
But, I realized after each time
that I mattered and my try is always worth it.

So Dear You,
Thank you for making me afraid.
Just know, I will keep trying again...
                           and again...
                                    and again.

Bonita

Look at her.
She is the reflection of perfection,
the perfect explanation of what beautiful is,
how She should always feel.

Yet her mirror...
Her mirror retaliates,
Reminding her not to forget, what She ate,
yesterday!
The minute that pleasure was added into the equation,
eating became an ingestion of insecurities and self-doubt.
All piled on her plate, accompanied by self-hate,
finding their way to her hips-
her hips, her thighs, her curves.

"Get a hold of yourself!" She says.
"How much could you have gained from the joy included in every
bite?"
Letting self-deprecation become an aftertaste,
She repeats to herself:
"A little extra doesn't make me any less.
A longer shirt will have to do it for today."

Her hair,
curls adorning her face,
curls with a mind of their own,
curls full of stories waiting to be told,
Strong.

Yet her mirror...
Her mirror stares back with a sinister smirk,
getting her fingers stuck under her waves,
hoping that her self-confidence drowns or goes away.

Breathe and look again.
Your curls represent information,
a carbon copy of your DNA,
coiled and rough,
like the road first travelled by your predecessors.
Your ancestors,
who had to get creative and fight,
so that you could inherit the right
to survive.
So that today you could represent them with pride.

So, fluff it up!
Your natural hair should not be adorned by shame.
It shouldn't even be a factor in the size of the smile
you give to the world each day.

Beauty is a feeling we get to know
and once we do, we own.
The secret to preservation is to hold on and never let go.

Bonita...
Empty your pockets,
Shake out the words,

The words you unconsciously hang on to self-mutilate.
Don't pay attention to what others have to say.
And, when the mirror starts acting up,
do not be afraid.

We are responsible for the images transposed
from the mirror into the brain.
And, when we don't like what we see,
we possess the power to change
until the image being seen and the one being relayed
become one and the same.

But it will start with those first words that you utter about yourself.
So, before you open your mouth, never forget
that God made you and God makes no mistakes!

10 Things I Would
Tell My Younger Self

1. Believe you can.
You will be surprised by the strength you will display
when nothing goes right.
When it all crumbles and you must put it all together,
you will shine.
There is fire in your eyes.

2. You will not break.
A woman's will is elastic and stretches until the fit is right.
At times, it will be tight but, like your favorite dress,
you will wear it with pride.
You will learn to dance in the rain with a tear
and a smile on your face.

3. You will not drown.
Life can feel like an ocean pulling you down
and keeps you fighting the waves,
until you learn that 60% of your body is water.
You have all you need to find your way.

4. You are the past.
The personified dream the ancestors had,
the give and take, the pride and pain,
the sacrifices they made
come full circle with you.

5. You are the future.
Not one race, but a collection of them, unified,
the "we are all the same",
the "you will knock me down",
and, like Maya, you will always rise.
Remember, there is fire in your eyes.

6. Respect yourself.
Your body is a temple, with your own religion:
only you decide who is worth bathing
in your holy waters – Heaven!
It's ok if you don't get there the first time.

7. You are loved.
Regardless of who breaks your heart,
there are those who will always have your back.
Not always your favorite people,
but the ones who are there no matter what.

8. You are enough.
Not everyone will appreciate what you bring to the table.
Don't be afraid to ask.
You deserve a full meal; never settle for a snack.

9. You are beautiful.
You will understand what that means
when you stop looking for yourself in others
and start to focus within.

10. You will be ok.
When it doesn't feel like it, continue reading.
Read this again
Believe you can!

Maddie Garcia

Open Letter to
My 14-Year-Old Self

I would like to start by saying I'm sorry.

I'm sorry I did not write to you sooner,
that I didn't find the courage to unmask
the fake behind your smile,
expose the sadness underneath
your teenage discrepancies,
or at least mitigate the pain that
at this very moment
suffocates the spirit that surrounds you.

Breathe.

Life is like a racetrack
in which negative and positive will always compete,
sometimes collide.
And when one is getting ready to win
the other will surprise you.
There will be highs and there will be lows,
big accomplishments and low blows
that will make you want to abandon
all that you have known.

But when you have cried that one last tear
(so you thought),
you will discover what it feels like to hurt.

You will try to carve the pain off your flesh,
creating openings in the hope
that you can bleed it away.

But instead,
your scars will serve as a reminder
of your strength,
of all you had to endure
and never want to go through again.

You will punish yourself,
equate the hunger in your heart
with the need to physically starve
in moments of desperation,
pile massive amounts of food on top
of the feelings and the shame
you are always trying to hide.
Filling you up inside,
it will all come out
and yes, it will hurt.

Not everyone will like you
but the worst pain will come
from hating yourself.
Looking in the mirror will trigger words
that feel more like bullets
you aim at your head.
You will want to die
but instead, let it hurt.

You will be surrounded by doubt
but you will do all the things you always wanted to do,
things that
'don't get done by people with bodies that look like you'.

You will conquer the hurt.

You will create life.
Your little ones will look up to you for guidance
and, while teaching them, you will learn.

Yes, you will learn.
That every masterpiece
starts out as a rough draft,
that the Creator has molded you
with His very own hands
as His vision of perfect
because you are.
And you will be perfect.
Not in the sense that there will be no imperfections,
but you will learn
that everything that makes you different
is what sets you apart from the rest.
You will change your outer appearance
over and over again,
in the hopes of a rebirth.

Until you learn
that changing the wrapper on a package
does not change the content inside.
Inside will be the only constant in your life
and regardless of what you look like,
how you feel about yourself will determine
the size of the beautiful smile
that makes you shine.
You will learn to smile even when you cry.

I'm sorry I did not reach out to you sooner.
But I want you to know that you will be beautiful
because you have been beautiful all along.

No One In Your Lifetime Could Ever Love You More...

Maddie Garcia

Letter to My Unborn

You and I
Connected
An extension of the same

Your vision is blurry and movements controlled
but your special bubble is guarded
by unconditional love.

Connected, unlike any other beings,
two living as one.
Although for a limited time,
the experience is indescribable.

Every day for you is an adventure,
living in that space,
discovering yourself,
wondering how the changes keep happening.

Well, Mommy has the same concerns.
My life will never be the same.
Because even without meeting,
you have already changed me.

What other people translate as a thump,
is my heartbeat whispering words
in a language only we can understand.

I want you to know, when our day comes,
and you no longer hear the words in my thump,
I hope you recognize the heart in my voice.

For it is me,
waiting patiently until we meet.
This time, with eyes wide open.

To give you an idea,
this love goes to infinity and beyond,
anywhere out of the world
to the galaxy that surrounds us.

And the day I finally hold you,
multiply all that times four!
No one in your lifetime
will ever love you more!

You and I
Connected
An extension of the same

I, your Mother and you, my Angel.

Maddie Garcia

A Vision of She

She stole my heart since the first day we met
and my life has never been the same.

She gave me a reason to believe
that it is ok to dream.

She made me look at life in different ways.
Impossible became I'm-possible, because of my baby girl.

Sometimes I'm not sure of my role in this world,
but I know I was born to be her mom.

Parents are meant to protect their kids,
but she was sent from God to save me.

She looks up to me to see what is
and I look to her for what will be.

Maddie Garcia

She - God's Gift

I always wanted a daughter that looked just like me,
never imagining how perfect she'd turn out to be.
Not because there is any resemblance,
but because of who she is.

Rough around the edges,
not always easy to take in
because she feels entitled to say everything;
she feels out loud.

Her heart screams out,
always causing a scene,
making it easy to know her
and for those who hurt her
to hear her tears.

But she is beautiful,
like I could never dream her to be,
holding the best side of daddy
and the interesting side of me.

She is not perfect
but she is God's gift,
to me.

I can only hope she realizes how especial she really is.

Looking at her, I take her in,
knowing deep in my heart
she is mine, but she is not me.

She is her own strong, stubborn person.
After all,
she does get that from me.

She Is

There is something
in the way she makes me look at life,
like there are no steps I'm unable to climb,
no skies unable to call mine.

In my eyes,
She is the brightest star of all
and I encourage her to never let go
of the universe.

Life is nothing but a dream that,
as impossible as it seems,
does exist.

I am a witness
to the best miracle of all,
my heart in completion mode
since the first time I felt your heartbeat.

You are this independent part
of my insides
that I get to watch blossom
on the outside
With daily reminders of YES,
you are mine.

I was told I gave you life to discover on my own,
that you were sent from above, to save mine.

You are forever my first love.

If today my life went completely wrong,
I would smile, happily knowing
I will forever be your mom.

Maddie Garcia

She - Mirror

When I look in this mirror,
it is the only time I like what I see:
my refined features and eagerness to live.
I smile, then I blink, for it is not me I see.

It is all She.

I have this idea of what the world could be
but she has her own views,
as if she lived 100 years before me.
Yet, we connect.

An extension of me,
the world maybe falling but
she is stronger than she knows.

She comes from fight and hope.

Determined,
so she will never be told where she belongs.

In her eyes there is fire.
In her hands, she cradles the desire
to be her own.

I accept that even when I'm no longer around,
we will always be one.
When she speaks,
my voice will echo at her will

For in this mirror, I see not what I am
but what I always dreamed to be,
a better version of me.

That, in reality,
is all She.

She

She,
the woman you have yet to meet.
The future only a mother can see.

Don't take your eyes off the prize.
Rather, let your mind accept and internalize
the divine,
the beauty,
that exists not only on the outside
but in being smart.

Let your eyes shine with the confidence
that no man or woman can deny.
Don't let anyone interrupt your cry.

It is your right to be heard, My Princess.
I know you still don't see it.

How can the mountains deviate to make space
for the path that you have yet to conquer?
How can you fight the demons that have traveled from the past;
hiding in your blood stream, reflecting on your skin, pushing
and making you believe that you have nothing else to give?

You will be surprised.
The solution is intertwined with the problems, hiding inside.

You come equipped with the antidote to your own venom.

You just have to believe that you are fierce and strong,
resilience, part of your bones.
The mountains will bow when the right time comes
to claim your throne.

You just have to listen, to the reflection of She,
the woman you will become,
the woman you have yet to meet,
the queen that's patiently waiting
for My Princess to become She.

She - A Love Letter
to My Daughter

You are my first love. I can't explain...
The first time I saw you,
I knew I was no longer a little girl.

I had to become the woman I would want you to be
Because when I see you, I see me.

You came from love and filled my life with joy.
Scary, I won't lie.
You have been the biggest challenge in my life

Yet, in you, there's hope, new dreams,
all the things I always wanted
but didn't get a chance to fulfill.

I know you must be your own self,
with your own failures and success.
That, no matter what I say,
you must pave your own way.

All I'm asking is
for you to slow down and observe:
You will never have all the answers
and it's OK to fail, as long as you learn.

Nothing in life is given.
Accomplishments must be earned
and your body is a treasure
that can bring new life to earth.

All you touch can be transformed.
Believe it with your heart
and never forget to love.
Don't forget to dream.
For dreams hold the key to unfolding new worlds
yet to be seen.

Dreams become thoughts,
thoughts become words
that can be spoken into existence.
People will say no.
But you must never give up.
Great things will happen when you are persistent.

When you feel you've given it your all,
that there is nowhere else to go,
don't give in to resistance.
Think of me,
bring out the fire within.
Always be consistent.

If I'm no longer here,
just look at yourself in the mirror
Search within my words for assistance.
Smile.
See the twinkle in your eyes, complete
and filled with pride in the distance.
You'll see traces of me.

For you will finally have become the woman
I've always known you would be.

My first love, you have my heart
and you always will.

Maddie Garcia

She - Unconditional

I finally learned what people mean when they say:
'Our children's lives are not ours to live.'
We only give them life.

Tasked to provide them the tools they need
to be able to fight their own battles
and (hopefully) live their best life,

our job becomes to watch from the sidelines,
praying we did enough.

Sometimes,
our hearts will lie:
make us believe we did better
than what transpires outside
that I am giving you the universe
when it's only my heart,
a mom wanting the very best for her child.

So, as I watch from afar, looking inward
to self-analyze what the mirror reflects,
I want to say:

I'm sorry
for everything you feel you didn't get.
I thought I had covered all the basics,
but it was my mistake.

I hope you know,
while not everything was perfect,
everything was smothered in love,
unconditional,
the best part of my world.

They say babies pick their parents before their birth.
I want to thank you for trusting me to be your mother.
I'm just a human full of flaws who loves you
since way before anything made sense.

Now remember

Life may throw you some curves.
That's when you look in the mirror and flaunt them
how I know you can.
Some people will want to hurt who you are.
That's when you show them the
strength you carry inside.

When you are out there
swinging your sword
and you hit the lowest of lows,
regardless of what happens in your world

always remember,
you are perfect to your mom.

She: I Have Her Back

From the beginning,
I helped her stand,
got to hold her hand,
kissed her pain goodbye.

Or at least,
transferred it out of her heart
and parked in mine, holding my breath
until she smiled again.

Now, I get to see her be,
to see her shine from within,
the light exuding from her eyes,
the affirmation when she says, "I Am!"
to take a stand.

No longer needing my voice to speak,
her vocal cords reflect from deep within me
and fragments of my life are edged into
her words

Now, as I hand her to the world,
as she develops her palate for right and wrong,
I watch her transform,
reach for new horizons and walk on her own.
She is strong.

I hope she knows.
There will always be traffic on the road,
stones trying to trip her when life tells her to run.
And, if she falls

(Or I should say when she falls),
it's just to give her a different view of the world
from the bottom up.

I hope she learns,
That, in life, situations have more than one approach.
And failure?
It's just a reminder to be humble.
That there is nothing wrong with reaching behind
or just falling back.

For there I stand with open arms.
I will always have her back.

Maddie Garcia

She - Eighteen

This year,
I will lose you to the next to last of his kind.
Out of all of them, he is the worst one.

Before him,
you are almost ready.
But after him,
you will be all in, full throttle.

He will lie and make you believe
that you could do all you want.
Not because it is feasible
but because no one will stand in your way.
What he doesn't say,
is that from now on
you are in it, alone.

Every decision you make
will be on your own.
And the consequences
will have to be accepted,
perhaps celebrated.
All responsibility lies on you.

Everything you have learned
throughout your teens
will be the resources you will use
to make something out of nothing.
Or one big thing out of everything,
no longer a little girl.

This year,
I will try to be prepared to lose you
to the next to last of its kind
and hope you have learned to fight
from all you have seen in me.

You will no longer be a kid.
You won't need mommy
On this,
your first young adult birthday
when you turn eighteen.

Maddie Garcia

There Is Nothing I Would Change...

Strong Women
(Four Generations)

Look at her.
Sitting tall and smiling halfway,
you would never guess
her tiny frame was far from frail.
She was made with an iron cast,
meant to keep out despair
while holding in the fight.
The flame of courage that would raise
if you even dared to shake the walls
she made strong with her tiny frame.
Abuela!

Look again.
Her reflection is the definition of strength,
the bird freed from its cage
courting new horizons.
She takes what she doesn't know
and turns doctored language into common words
to make possibility of the unexpected.
She is my center, my Mother!

Don't look at her but look through her.
Carrying a universe inside,
equal amounts of truths and lies
feed her insecurities,
trying to undo the progress running through her veins.
Fire and strength,
she is special but doesn't believe it yet.
She has been assigned to explode,
to burn the world with her sun,
letting the particles of many lives
write themselves into history.
My story.

Look beyond her smile,
to the innocence every human desires,
the overflow of hope.
Her pain accounted for,
her power, a tiny seed at the core
of her undiscovered potential
as the strongest link
in this connection of four.
There's much to be accomplished,
her future is only a projection,
my Baby Girl.

She is life that gave life to this life I'm living.
How could I have known the day that I was born
that I would pass down the gift of life through this lineage?
Having a daughter, reason enough for living,
we are all She,
strong women existing within one another.

Maddie Garcia

Love At First Sight

I never believed in love at first sight.
It is one of those myths that people over recite.

Like, I can't remember my life before you.
You take my breath away with every look; like,
I want to be better because of you.

I once thought that I could spot a fake
and all explanations were plastic behind that phrase,
until I encountered your face.

My entire life flashed before my eyes,
analyzing how I would explain all the bad
so you could be proud of who I am.

There are no combinations of the alphabet that can describe
the feelings I carry inside,
the fears I constantly wish I could subside,
the evil I am willing to fight
so it never finds a way into your life.

My life isn't any longer about me.
Guarding the doors of your world, my job
to watch you become the best that you can be.

It is as if
this shield that I've spent my existence covering in
is crumbling.

My weakest point
fully exposed,
becoming visible to the world.

Now everyone knows where I hurt.
You, my kryptonite
the quickest way to get me to die,
obvious.

The day you found your way into my arms,
you wrapped your fingers around my heart to claim me

I am forever yours and you are mine,
love at first sight.
You give meaning to who I am.

All overrated love phrases
are not eloquent enough
to paint a portrait of this love
that defines me.

You just remind me
every time you call me Mom.

Mother

"I love you Mommy,"
a very powerful phrase
creating the most compelling side effects known to man.
If I could bottle it as a substance
I would have millions in my hands.

It's our version of Kryptonite,
Making you super
and weak,
all at once.

You see,
as it enters your blood stream
it almost stings,
bringing tears to your eyes,
accelerating your heartbeat,
and creating weakness at your knees.

Your stomach sinks.
The emotions bounce
before you can swallow
and you just want to scream!

With a smile, of course.

It's like a powerful drug.
Once it goes into your blood stream
it is absorbed by your cells.
Your body acquires new strength,
superpowers you never expected.

At the sight of a fall,
you become Flash,
moving from one room to the other
with the speed of light,
just to soften the land.

You become Hulk,
growing super muscles
at the sight of a threat.

Like a Thunder Cat,
you scream and yell
marking the territory you protect.

You develop Spider senses,
internal alarms going off
at a stretch of silence.

You become The Man in Black,
roaming the nights,
trying to erase bad memories
from their minds

Wishing you could become Professor X,
to get inside their heads,
to let them know and feel that all will be ok.

Even though you are the most complex of all Heroes,
you sometimes forget
you are Humble, Unbelievable MAN

Super Mom - the most intricate hero,
is more than a man.
She is a Wondrous Outstanding -MAN!!!!

Yes, I AM!

But I'm content with being called Mom,
with receiving those tender hugs and kisses before bed,
with seeing you flourish into spectacular boys
and my awesome girl.
It is the reason why I become normal again.

Superpowers vanish.
(But just until I need them again.)
For now, I'm extremely proud to be known
as your mother.

They

They make me laugh.
They make me cry.
They give meaning to the phrase
'What was I thinking',
more often than not.

They test my patience,
making me regret not waiting 10 more years
before having them.

They forever scarred my body
and changed me inside out.
They became the nagging pain
that I can't be without.

They are all different
and overwhelm me the same.
But, if I had to do it all over,
there is nothing I would change.

Who would have known,
that little kisses and smiles
is all it would take
to drown my heart with love
and hit my mind with reset?
Everyday.

I am doctor. I'm a counselor. I'm a friend.
I'm even the perfect pillow
when they need to rest.
I'm no longer human.
I am a Mom.

They make it possible for me
to know who I am.

Maddie Garcia

A Knock on the Door

Every day I watch you grow,
become someone
that even I want to know,

Someone I want the world to see.
Pride exploding from my chest,
I can't wait for you to just be.

But first, I must learn to let go,
to undo the lace extending from my arms,
nicely shaped into your back.

And this is hard.
I have wiped every tear that you've cried.
Every time you failed
I encouraged you to try, to fight.
'Cause I'm your number one fan.

Understand,
you are mine to protect,
to nurture, to direct,
to make you believe what I see in you
each time you look at yourself.

The day will come when the ties will be cut,
independence will be known.
You will become hungry for the world.

Then, I will have to let you go.

I just hope that you never forget;
I will always be more than a friend.
When you need a helping hand
or just an ear to vent,
don't hesitate to dial.

From my love there will always be an encore.
No matter how high the tide rises,
your waters will always make it to my shore.

In other words,
I will always be your home waiting
for that knock on the door.

Maddie Garcia

May She Feel Special
In Every Way...

To My Oldest Niece
(Happy Sweet 16 to My Chachi)

She was the first to come into our lives.
She extended the love between generations an extra line.

She showed us another type of love.
She showed me connections I thought impossible.

She looks nothing like me,
yet I see me in who she is.
She will always be the first-
his first daughter, their first granddaughter, and my first niece.

In every stage of her life,
I wish her happiness and love.
Not the love that you feel for someone else
but the love you only find inside yourself.

For this love opens all the doors-
for us to love others
and for others to love us more.

May she always feel special in every way
and love herself as much as she possibly can.

May she savor the crazy ride we call life,
put her hands up when she falls
and be ready for the climb.

Lastly, I hope she knows
she is always in my thoughts,
that I will never be too far.
I'm just at the other end of the phone.

She - Once Upon a Dream

(For my niece Naillil, in her Mom's voice)

I thought I had seen her before,
Once upon a dream.
But I only saw what I wanted,
the way I had imagined my little girl to be.

The notion of perfect that had been indoctrinated in me,
I had a specific vision of how she was supposed to be:
loud, curious, touching everything,
bribing her to sit still.
Until I met her.

She defied every expectation of the norm:
calm, quiet, in her own world.

When others thought she wasn't learning,
she was absorbing it all.
When others thought she wasn't looking,
she was processing the moment
until she was ready to show off!

And she did.

I just hope
that she can look back one day and feel
that we could not have asked for a more special being
to complete the family that we are.

That she knows we are proud of every stone,
the ones stepped on and the ones picked up
to knock down walls-
the walls that tried to keep her contained.

That she has star dust running through her veins,
so shine my beautiful swan!

Shine, she does,
writing awards in fifth grade,
piano recitals from a young age,
becoming different characters
every time she steps on a stage,
memorizing all her lines,
plus the ones before and after that!

Make no mistake.
She is destined for greatness
just for being herself.

Baby girl,
Never change for anyone else!

Beautiful inside and out,
she showed me that perfect is not one thing,
not one size fits all. Not at all!
We make our own.

Better than any dream I could've ever had,
she is my beautiful reality!

Maddie Garcia

Warrior Princess
(For Aliyah's Sweet 16, in
her mother's voice)

There is nothing more special than
a mother-daughter bond.
This poem is for my Princess.
Love you always,
Mom

Every castle needs a princess
who will grow up to be a Queen.
I always knew I wanted a family.
So, I married a King.

First, God blessed us with our own Prince Charming
who lit up our world.
Then, She came into our lives, like the perfect storm.

She was feisty from the beginning,
making decisions from the womb,
arriving on her own time,
not when the doctors were telling her to.

End of the week, on a Friday, at 11:56 am,
I held her in my arms for the first time
and my life has never been the same.

I should have guessed from the beginning
we were in for a wild ride.
But my heart was overwhelmed trying to make sense
of all this love I was feeling inside.

There has never been a challenge
that she hasn't faced head on.
Proving to us that anything is possible
since the moment she arrived in the world.

She was diagnosed with ADHD at only 4 years old.
To some a disability, to her;
her world just moved faster than ours.

She is loud.
She pops,
splashes of pinks and rainbows bright.

She is kind, with a heart of gold.
There's too much life inside of her
to spend it sitting down.

Tumbling from side to side,
balancing her energy,
every floor like in gymnastics, an exercise,
full of surprises!

Until one day,
She faced the toughest judge of all.
At 14, her life came down to one last vault.
She jumped!

Death looked her in the eyes
and for a moment
thought it had earned another soul.

In the midst of it all,
our family questioned 'Why Us?
We have a perfect family!
And now She is being taken from us?!'

A rare cervical tumor,
the doctors as baffled as us.
Every second was a gift.
Every breath, precious.

She was our source of strength.
Every day was difficult
but she pushed through,
with a smile on her face.
Her music never stopped;
she danced her way through.

I hope she knows with each day that passes,
She is loved,
and an inspiration to all of us,
a fire with a built-in spark plug,
Daddy's little girl.
And to me,
She will always be a hero.

We can't wait to see her blossom into
the amazing woman she will be,
the future Queen of this castle,
our Warrior Princess.

Maddie Garcia

To My Daughter's Unborn Baby Girl

(For the Rios Family, in Grandma's voice to her Granddaughter)

The day will come
when you will take your first breath.
Your vision will be foggy
and sounds not as pleasant.

Yet, the vibrant colors of the world will speak.
You will discover rainbows, see shapes.
All the letters of the alphabet will scrabble to form your name.

You will exist in a world
without boundaries, without limits,
where love won't be a word but a verb.

I want to be prepared
when you ask, 'Who am I?'
so I can say:

You are the product of a dream
us, me, you, we
the dream I see
whenever I look at my little girl.

When she holds you in her arms,
don't be alarmed.
She'll be flooded with tears representing rivers of hope
accumulated in her heart,
meant to protect you, to guide you.

You are so special
because you will make my little girl a mom,
a woman
elevating our connection an extra step.

I never thought my heart could expand enough
to harbor what's inside me,
to be able to experience an extension of who I am,
a version of a better me reflected in my daughter's eyes.
But to see you, to hold you, to feel you
will be like no other love.

I wish I had the perfect melody to sing you the perfect song
on how this feels,
how my maternal instincts Hiroshima imagining
your sweet face, Baby Girl!

I can't wait for the day when I get to tell you, face to face,
that you are the reality of my dreams,
my daughter's daily reminder of selfless affection,
the love I feel for her multiplied without question,

a ripple of love,
as the stone hops
from mine to hers to your heart.

A product of a dream,
You are me, us.
You are we.

Maddie Garcia

My Favorite Star
(For Ishana, in her Mother's voice)

"Twinkle, twinkle little star
how I wonder where you are.
Up above the world so high
My own diamond in the sky
Like a traveler in the dark
I am thankful for your spark."

My star...

Sometimes,
I listen,
waiting for the slightest sound
as I open the box of
'I need to remember'

And I swear,
I hear the smile in your voice,
the innocence in your words,
the gasping 'I love you'
as the air escaped your lungs.

That...
I want to forget,

this grief that overwhelms our lives.
Your life was taken before its time
and I miss you my Little Star.

The first time I held you,
I saw the twinkle in your eyes.
I could not believe that you were mine.
It was as if all my needs and wants
had been packaged into a little life
and my job was to guard it.

I was blessed with the honor
of having you as my daughter.

As your mother,
I was meant to teach you and guide you.
Little did I know,
you held the lessons inside you.
I was just privileged to watch you.

You taught me about right and wrong,
unconditional love,
how some things seem good in your head
but feel different when done.
Our actions affect more than just us.

You, the biggest star of all,
the center of my world
the refined version of me
that was meant to conquer the world...

There are days
I feel my reflection has been turned off.
In the mirror there is a void
only your smile used to fill.

But I swear, I feel you all around me
in the most basic smells,
in the smile of your friends,
in the songs we loved to dance to, in a funny way.

Today,
I've decided not to cry.
I have grown tired of asking why,
being mad at God, and hating my so-called life
without you.

Instead, I want to...

I want to do the things we used to do,
skip work and ditch school,
eat ice cream and talk about you.

In the hopes, I can energize your light
so you never forget to shine.
Because I know,
I know,
this is not it.

Your twinkle was too strong to remain in your eyes.
So, God chose a bigger venue
And He...
He gave you the sky.

I will see you again.

But until then,
peeking through my window at night,
I hope to find you
causing chaos amongst the stars.

Because that is who you are.
Twinkle.
Twinkle!
My Favorite Star!

colophon
Brought to you by Wider Perspectives Publishing, care of James Wilson, with the
mission of advancing the poetry and creative community of Hampton Roads,
Virginia.

See our production of works from ...

Chichi Iwuorie
Symay Rhodes
Tanya Cunningham-Jones
(Scientific Eve)
Terra Leigh
Ray Simmons
Samantha Borders-Shoemaker
Bobby K.
(The Poor Man's Poet)
J. Scott Wilson (TEECH!)
Charles Wilson
Gloria Darlene Mann
Neil Spirtas
Edith Blake
Jorge Mendez & JT Williams
Sarah Eileen Williams
Stephanie Diana (Noftz)
the Hampton Roads
Artistic Collective

Jason Brown (Drk Mtr)
Martina Champion
Tony Broadway
Zach Crowe
Ken Sutton
Crickyt J. Expression
Lisa M. Kendrick
Cassandra IsFree
Nich (Nicholis Williams)
Samantha Geovjian Clarke
Natalie Morison-Uzzle
Gus Woodward II
Patsy Bickerstaff
Catherine TL Hodges
Jack Cassada
Dezz
Grey Hues
Jade Leonard
... and others to come soon.

We promote and support the artists of the 757
from the seats, from the stands,
from the snapping fingers andclapping hands
from the pages, and the stages
and now we pass them forth
to the ages

Check for the above artists on
FaceBook, the Virginia Poetry
Online channel on YouTube,
and other social media.

Made in the USA
Middletown, DE
08 February 2022

59894405R00050